NICKY & VERA

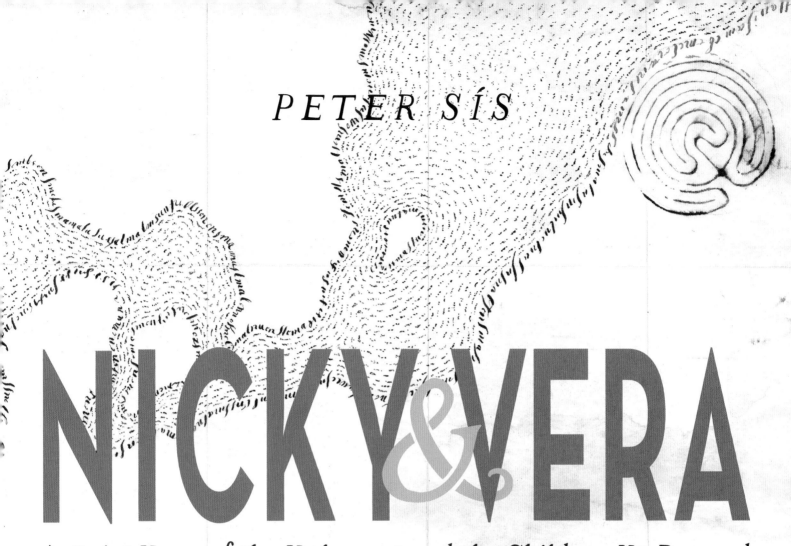

PETER SÍS

NICKY&VERA

A Quiet Hero of the Holocaust and the Children He Rescued

Norton Young Readers
An imprint of W. W. Norton & Company
Independent Publishers Since 1923

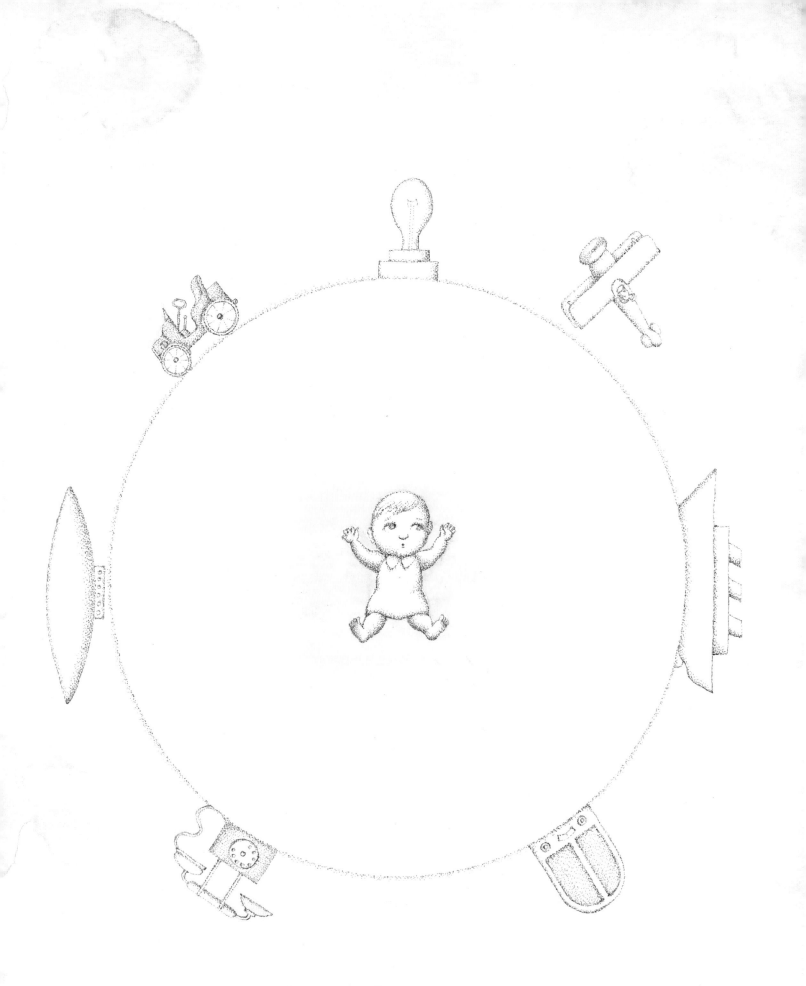

Nicky was born in 1909,

into a century full of promise.

At Nicky's school, the students were encouraged to follow their interests, whatever they were.

Nicky discovered he liked mathematics, stamp collecting, photography, and fencing.

The students had all kinds of pets.
Nicky raised pigeons.

It didn't matter what the students were interested in, so long as they were interested in something.

As a young man, Nicky traveled all over Europe.

He worked as a banker.

He learned German and French; how to ride a motorcycle, drive a car, and fly a plane.

He was an expert fencer, on an Olympic team.

Nicky and his friends talked about politics. They worried about the situation in Europe. In Germany, the Nazi party, led by Adolf Hitler, was building an army.

In December 1938, Nicky planned to take a skiing vacation, but a friend called.

"Come to Prague," he said.

In 1938, Vera was ten years old.

She lived with her family in a small town near the big city of Prague.

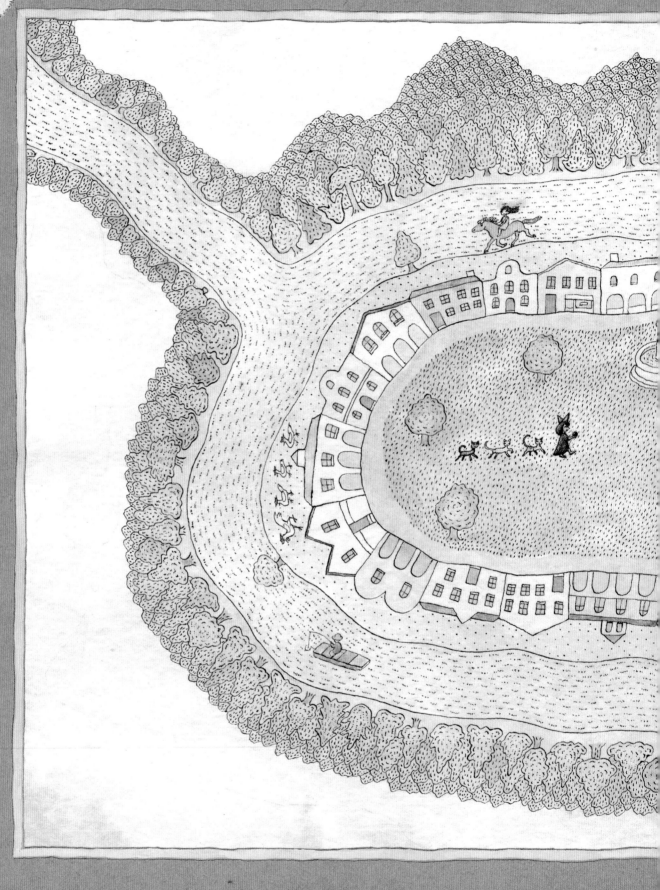

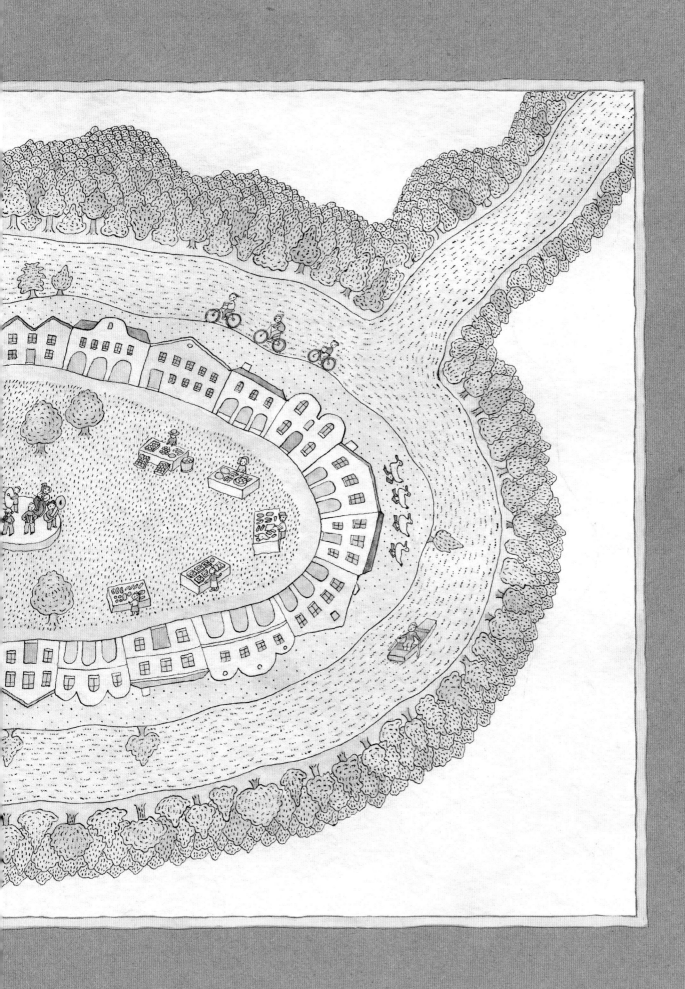

Vera was the Queen of Cats.

She would adopt a stray whenever she found one.

She loved to feed
the horses that
pulled the wagon
for her parents'
business.

It was a happy childhood.

They were
one of the few
Jewish families
in town.
It made no
difference.
They were all
friends.

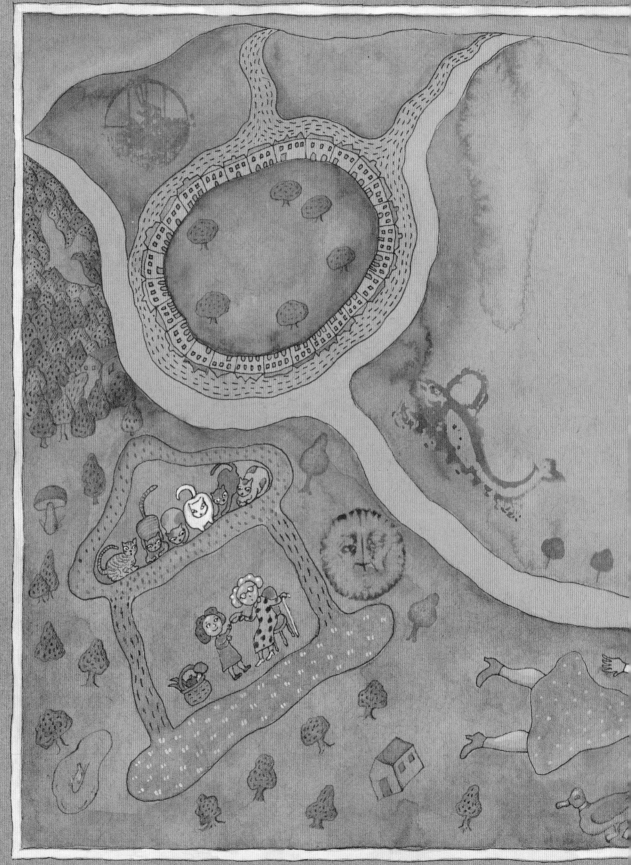

Vera helped
her almost blind
grandmother
when she
came to visit.
Vera's
grandmother
remembered
Vera's face
by touching it.

citizens of the young republic of Czechoslovakia.

Sometimes when the family visited cousins in Prague, they went to synagogue.

Vera's family spoke Czech. But if her parents wanted to share secrets, they spoke German to each other.

In October, the German army marched into the

People afraid of the Germans ran with everything they could take.

One morning there was a new girl in Vera's class. Vera gave her an extra pair of shoes. "I had no time to take anything," the barefoot girl said.

In the family's cellar and barn there was suddenly extra food and clothing. "Just in case," said Vera's mother.

border region of Czechoslovakia, called Sudetenland.

When visiting Prague, Vera's mother heard about an Englishman who was helping children leave Czechoslovakia to escape the Germans.

She discussed it with Vera's father and they decided that Vera should go to England.

Nurenberg

Annexation of Austria

The Englishman was Nicky.

Munich Agreement

Kristallnacht

He saw that war was near,
and something had to be done.
England would allow refugees under
seventeen to come—if families could be
found to take care of them and travel
could be arranged.

Nicky set up an office in a hotel in Prague.

He made lists of children.
He took their photographs.
He found train connections.

Spies kept watch.

In January, Nicky returned to London.

In the evenings after work, he placed advertisements in the newspapers to find foster families to take care of the children.

He applied for visas and made travel arrangements.
Sometimes he paid with his own money and made his own stamps.

There wasn't much time.

In March 1939, the German army

invaded the rest of Czechoslovakia.

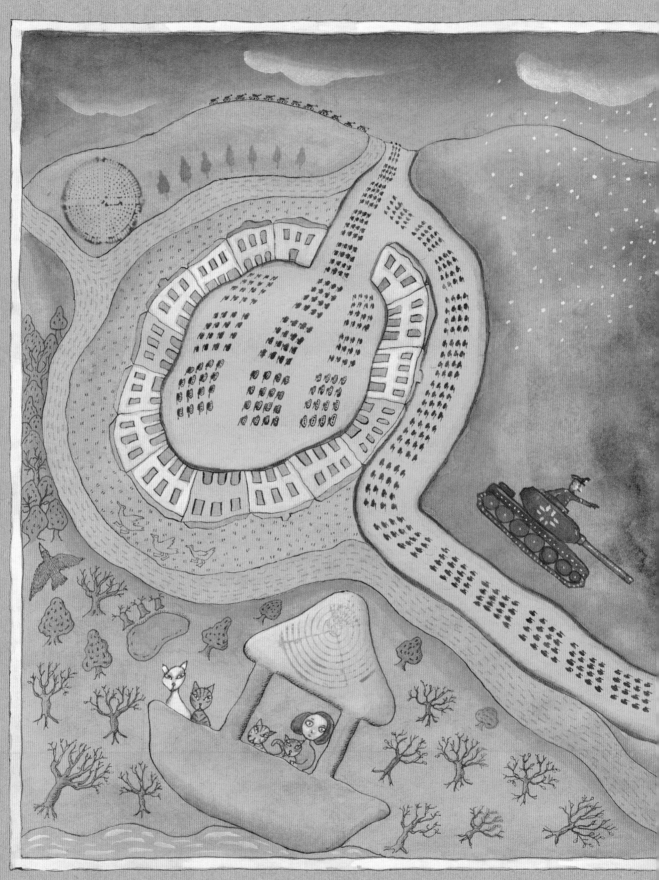

through Vera's hometown.

One of them came to the family house and said he would be moving in. He told them to stop speaking Czech.

Vera's father refused. Vera vowed that she would never speak German.

The day came for Vera to leave.

She packed her clothes.

Vera's father gave her a diary. He told her to write down her memories, until she could return home and see them again.

*She said
goodbye
to her
grandparents.*

She said goodbye to her cousins, who were to follow her to England on a later train.

Seventy-six children got on the train.

Vera tried not to cry.

She and the other children
did not know what lay ahead.
So they told stories
about the lives they left behind.

After three days and nights, they arrived in London.

The rest of the children were picked up.
Vera waited in the empty hall.

Finally, her new family came.

Eight trains left Prague in the spring and summer of 1939.

Six hundred sixty-nine children of all ages reached London safely.

On September 1, Germany attacked Poland.

That day, the ninth train, carrying 250 children, including Vera's cousins, was due to leave Prague. But the borders were closed and the train never left.

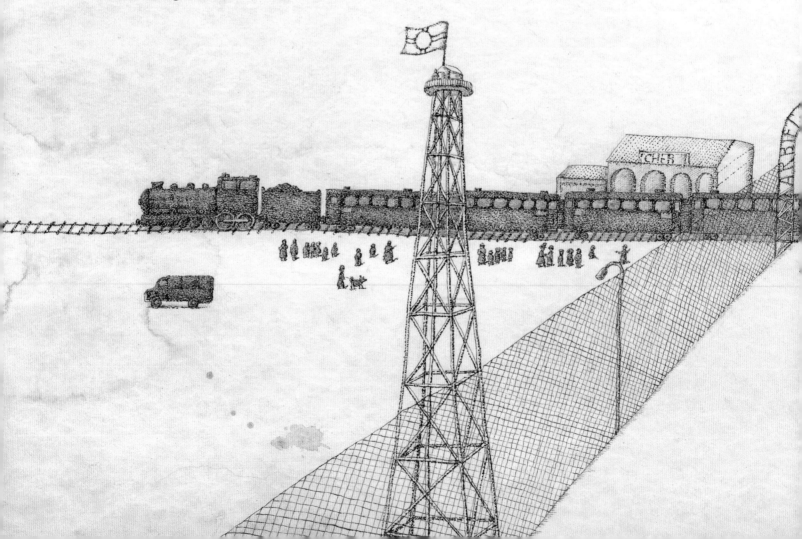

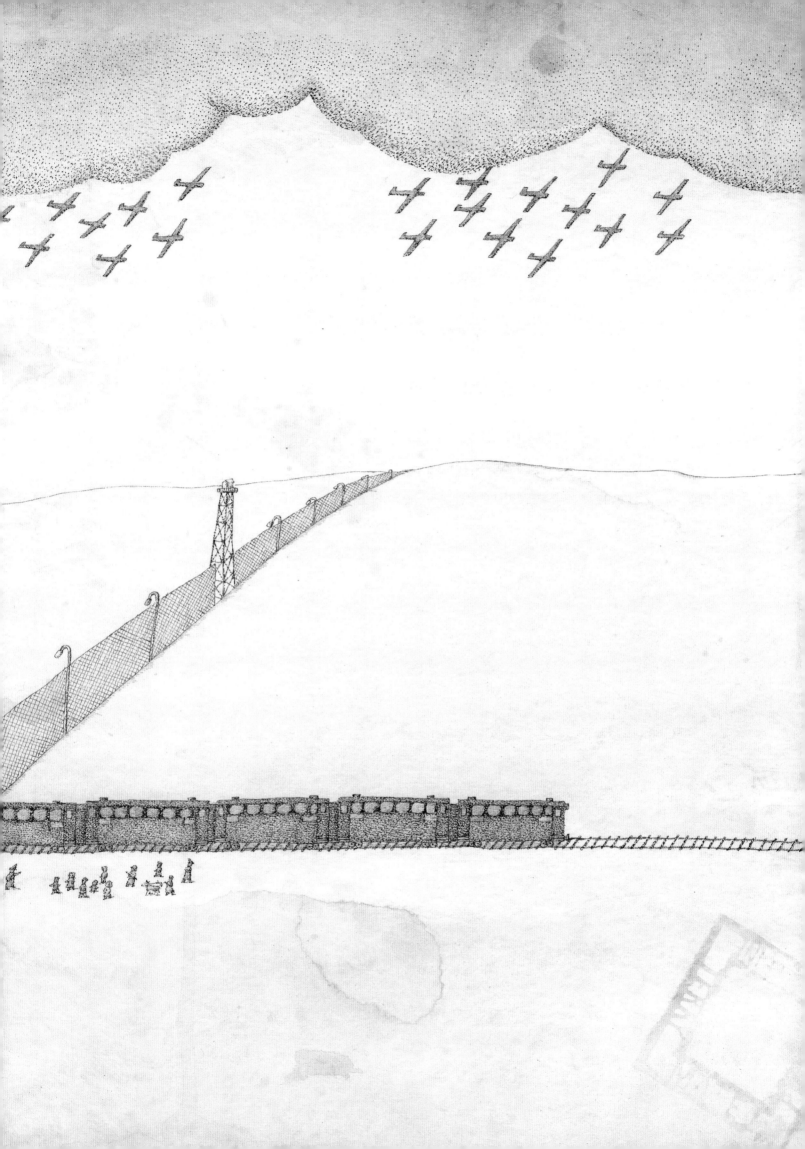

Nicky was out of time.

He put away his records.

He served in the war as an
ambulance driver.

He was evacuated by boat
from the French city of
Dunkirk as the German
army advanced.

Vera wrote in her diary every day.

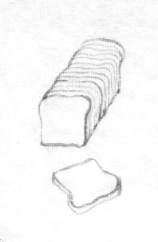

She learned a new language.

She went to a new school, and learned to eat new foods.

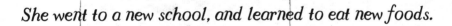

The war was everywhere. She had no news from home. She hoped her parents were safe.

When the war was over, Vera went back to her town.

Her family
was gone.

Her father and
mother had died
in the Nazi camps.
Her cousins too.
She only found the
daughter of one of
her old cats.

She did not stay in Czechoslovakia.

After four years, she returned to England.

She got married and had a family.

Nicky lived quietly.

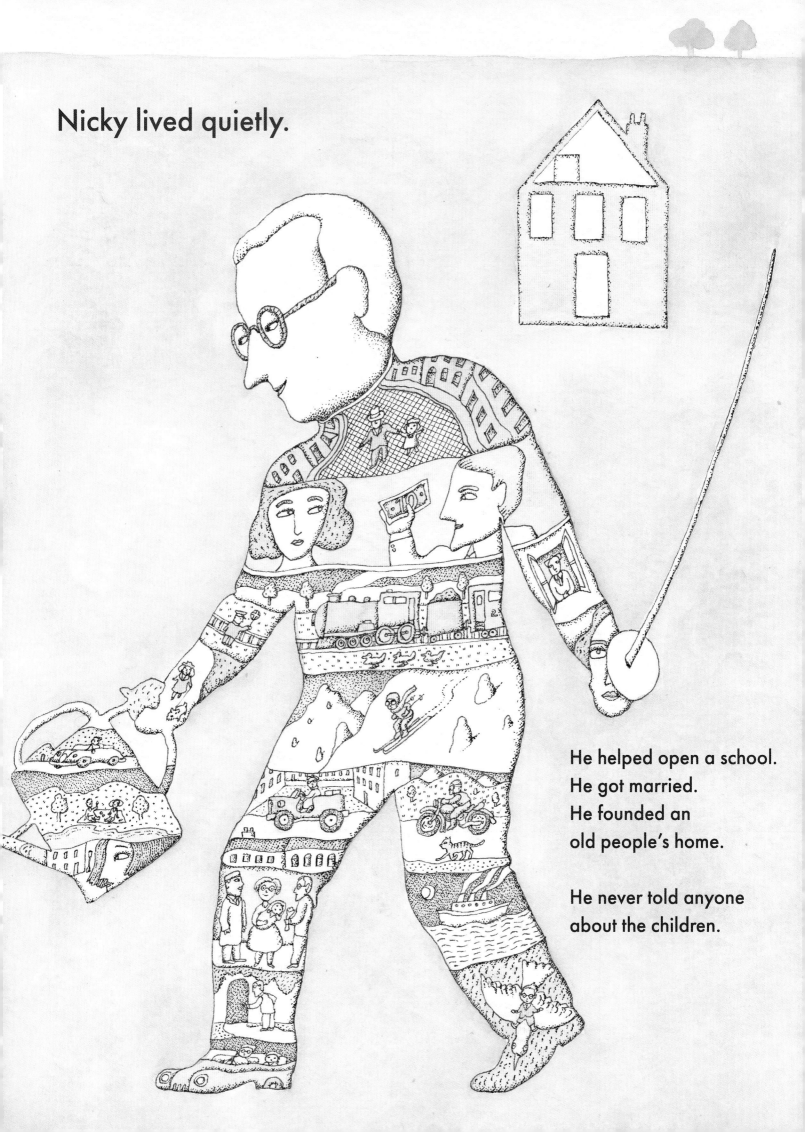

He helped open a school.
He got married.
He founded an
old people's home.

He never told anyone
about the children.

When Nicky was an old man,
his wife found the records.

One day, he got a phone call. Did he want to meet some people he used to know?

Vera got a phone call, too. Did she want to meet some old friends?

Nicky was the guest on a television show.

He didn't know it, but the old friends
he had been invited to meet were some of the children.

Vera was one of them.
She sat next to Nicky. When the host told her story, she stood up.

Everyone stood up.

669 children would not have survived

if not for Nicky, who went to Prague and saved their lives.

I was not a hero, Nicky said.

I did not face any danger, as real heroes do.

I only saw what needed to be done.

Author's Note

Fathers and sons talk about all kinds of things. When my son Matej was fifteen we took a trip to Prague, where I grew up, and talked about heroes: what it takes to be a hero—a real hero, a sports hero, an ancient hero, a people's hero. Walking around Prague one day we found ourselves at the National Museum (decorated with the names of Czech national heroes). The marble lobby of the museum was full of cheerful people who were getting ready to cut a giant cake decorated with a chocolate train and the words WINTON TRAIN. It was a celebration of the 100th birthday of Nicholas Winton. Some of the cheering people were "children" he had rescued from Prague, who were about to get on a train to take the same journey to London that they had taken some seventy years earlier. Nicholas Winton was to meet them there at the Liverpool Street train station. We watched, we listened, and we learned the whole story. That was our introduction to a real hero.

As a child in postwar Czechoslovakia I had heard many fragments of stories about how people had survived. I had met people who mentioned that their parents lived in London or had been on the trains, and a friend I went to school with in Prague later wrote to tell me that her oldest sister had been on Winton's list and was supposed to leave for London. "One day before the departure my mother decided to remove her name from the list," she wrote. "She could not get used to the idea that her nine-year-old daughter would travel alone into the unknown. Shortly after that, my mother and older sister were both transported to Terezín concentration camp. They both survived. On the plus side, if there is any, the fact that my sister did not get on the train made it possible for another child to leave—and so they both survived, but under different conditions."

Matej and I realized that these events touched our lives more closely than we had imagined. I was always looking up to the celebrated adventurers, explorers, inventors, and dreamers. But I had not paid enough attention to the reluctant and quiet heroes. After all, Winton did not speak about what he had done until 1989. We have learned about his actions from the films of Matej Minac and the books of Vera Gissing and Ivan K. Backer—and from the news media, after he made a famous appearance on BBC television. Here was a man who would see something wrong and do something to correct it, but who never claimed to be a hero.

Nicholas Winton was born in London on May 19, 1909. His parents were of German Jewish origin and had emigrated to England and converted to Christianity. Nicholas attended Stowe boarding school, near London, which had recently opened, and which offered a modern education. While at Stowe, Nicholas took up the sport of fencing. Later he would be selected for the British national team for the Olympics, but the games were canceled when the Second World War broke out.

After graduation, Nicholas worked for banks in Hamburg, Berlin, and Paris before returning to London to become a stockbroker. At the end of 1938 he planned to take a ski vacation with a friend, Martin Blake; but Blake asked to meet in Prague instead. In October that year, Germany occupied the border area of Czechoslovakia called the Sudetenland, and in November Jewish homes and businesses in Germany and Austria were attacked on a night known as "Kristallnacht." By December, Prague was filled with as many as 250,000 Czech and Jewish refugees living with few resources in freezing conditions. There, Blake introduced Nicholas to Doreen Warriner and Trevor Chadwick, who were organizing the British Committee for Refugees from Czechoslovakia to provide help. The British government would accept refugees under seventeen years old, providing they had a family to host them, and £50 for a return ticket, so they could be repatriated when the crisis was over. There were organizations that arranged for the evacuation of children from Germany and Austria (known as "kindertransport"), but not from Czechoslovakia. In Prague, Nicholas realized there was too much bureaucracy and too little time. He began taking names and photographs. As word got around, lines of parents—desperate to get their children to safety—formed outside his hotel room.

Nicholas Winton

After three weeks in Prague, Nicholas returned to London. With the help of his mother, he placed advertisements for host families in the newspapers, raised money, and applied to the government for entry permits for the children. When the government was slow to issue permits, he forged them. Meanwhile, in Prague, Chadwick bribed railway officials, policemen, and even the head of the Gestapo (the German secret police) to allow children to leave. The first group left on March 14, 1939. Seven more groups followed, but on September 1, Germany invaded Poland, beginning World War Two. Borders were closed, and a ninth train, carrying 250 children, was not allowed to leave. It is believed that only two children from that train survived the war.

During the war, Nicholas served as an ambulance driver, and in 1940 he was surrounded and evacuated with the rest of the British army from the beaches at Dunkirk in France. After the war, he worked for the International Committee for Refugees, raising money for Jewish organizations, the International Bank in Paris, and for charities in Britain supporting disabled people and the elderly. While working in Paris, he met a Danish woman, Grete Gjelstrup. They married and had three children.

For almost fifty years, Nicholas told no one about the children he had helped to rescue. In 1988, Grete found scrapbooks he had kept containing their records. Nicholas thought they were of no interest and suggested that she throw them away. "You can't throw these papers away," she told him. "They are children's lives."* Grete contacted researchers to try and track down some of the children, which led to an invitation to Nicholas to appear on a popular television program, *That's Life*. Unknown to him, dozens of the children—now middle-aged or elderly—were in the studio audience. When the presenter asked, "Is there anyone here who owes their life to Nicholas Winton?" they stood.

Nicholas received many awards and honors, including honorary citizenship of Prague, presented to him by the president of the Czech Republic, Václav Havel. He died in 2015, at the age of 106.

One of "Winton's Children," as they have been called, was Veruška ("Vera") Diamantova, who has told her story in her own book, and in several interviews. Vera was born in 1928 and grew up in Celakovice, a small town outside Prague. On July 1, 1939, shortly before her eleventh birthday, she left Prague with her older sister, Eva, in the seventh group of children to travel to London. She stayed with a family in Liverpool and later attended a school for Czech refugees in Wales. Her father was shot after spending most of the war in a Nazi concentration camp. Her mother was imprisoned in the Auschwitz and Belsen concentration camps but survived the war; she died of typhus shortly afterward, before Vera was able to return. When Vera was sent back to Czechoslovakia in 1945, she found only an aunt—and the daughter of one of her cats, which had been adopted by a neighbor. The rest of her family had perished.

Vera left Czechoslovakia for England a second time in 1949, a year after the pro-Soviet Communist government took power in 1948. She remained there for the rest of her life. She married and had three children. Her book, *Pearls of Childhood*—based on her diaries—and the many interviews she has given are the inspiration for the story told in these pages.

Among the others of Winton's Children are film director Karel Reisz; Hugo Marom, a founder of the Israeli Air Force; geneticist Renata Laxova; poet Gerda Mayer; Milena Grenfell-Baines; and the politician Alfred Dubs. As a member of the British Parliament, Dubs advocated and sponsored legislation to protect and provide for migrant children during the European refugee crisis of 2015–16.

---

* Robert D. McFadden, "Nicholas Winton, Rescuer of 669 Children from Holocaust, Dies at 106," *New York Times*, July 1, 2015.

Resources

Backer, Ivan K. *My Train to Freedom: A Jewish Boy's Journey from Nazi Europe to a Life of Activism.* New York: Skyhorse Publishing, 2016.

Gissing, Vera. *Pearls of Childhood.* New York: St. Martin's Press, 1989.

Minac, Matej, dir. *The Power of Good: Nicholas Winton.* 2002.

"Vera Gissing—April 22, 2006." Interview by Dr. Sidney Bolkosly. Voice/Vision Holocaust Survivor Oral History Archive at the University of Michigan-Dearborn. http://holocaust.umd.umich.edu/gissing/

Winton, Barbara. *If It's Not Impossible . . . : The Life of Sir Nicholas Winton.* Kibworth, Leicestershire: Troubador Publishing, 2014.

Photograph of Nicholas Winton courtesy of Barbara Winton.

Copyright © 2021 by Peter Sís

Printed in China
First Edition

For information about permission to reproduce selections from this book, write to
Permissions, W. W. Norton & Company, Inc., 500 Fifth Avenue, New York, NY 10110

For information about special discounts for bulk purchases, please contact
W. W. Norton Special Sales at specialsales@wwnorton.com or 800-233-4830

Manufacturing by Worzalla
Book design by Peter Sís and Ann Bobco
Production manager: Julia Druskin

Library of Congress Cataloging-in-Publication Data

Names: Sís, Peter, 1949– author.
Title: Nicky & Vera : a quiet hero of the Holocaust and the children he rescued / Peter Sís.
Other titles: Nicky and Vera
Description: First edition. | New York, N.Y. : W. W. Norton & Company, Inc., 2021. |
    Includes bibliographical references. | Audience: Ages 6–8
Identifiers: LCCN 2020041100 | ISBN 9781324015741 (hardcover) | ISBN 9781324015758 (epub)
Subjects: LCSH: Winton, Nicholas, 1909–2015—Juvenile literature. | Righteous Gentiles in the Holocaust—
    Biography—Juvenile literature. | World War, 1939–1945—Jews—Rescue. | World War, 1939–1945—
    Children—Rescue. | Jewish children in the Holocaust—Juvenile literature.
Classification: LCC D804.66.W56 S57 2021 | DDC 940.53/1835092 [B]—dc23
LC record available at https://lccn.loc.gov/2020041100

W. W. Norton & Company, Inc., 500 Fifth Avenue, New York, N.Y. 10110
www.wwnorton.com

W. W. Norton & Company Ltd., 15 Carlisle Street, London W1D 3BS

0 9 8 7 6 5 4 3